My Carob Bar Recipes

by Oshri

BUTTERFLYON BOOKS

My Carob Recipes
By Oshri

Published by Butterflyon Books
Los Angeles
ISBN 979-8-218-12956-9

For anyone who's enjoyed NaamNom's Carob Bars, and for anyone who wants to align their sweet-tooth with their health.

Table of Contents

About the Journey

How did I start making NaamNom's Carob Bars?

Thank you for taking a look at these recipes!

I grew up in a home where everyone cooks and I've always loved making food and making up recipes. You couldn't grow up in my home and not be experienced in the kitchen— both of my parents led by example in that.

In my late 20's, a friend of mine was diagnosed with Lyme's Disease and her doctor recommended she no longer eat chocolate. I saw how disappointed she was about this and one day while I was at the supermarket, some carob powder caught my eye. I started experimenting and after a few iterations, I shared a carob bar with almonds and raisins with my friend and she loved it!

I started making them for more friends, bringing them along to dinners and potlucks. Eventually people started asking to buy them, some shops asked to carry them, and I was making a couple thousand or so bars a month. At the peak of wholesale activity (just before the Covid lockdown) they were at about 85 locations.

I made up to 10 flavors and had fun running the business for a while. Eventually, however, the business got to be exhausting in a way that did not feel as rewarding. My right-hand man in the kitchen, a man of tremendous reliability, heart, and the highest of standards, who was the only other person I trusted to make NaamNom's Carob Bars without me present (which was just a handful of times), also had a sudden health challenge and was incapacitated from work, which was also disheartening. Everything that went into these was so personal.

I didn't want to make bars that were not full of love, and I started to slow down, eventually coming to the conclusion that I still wanted to make the bars available (through their recipes), but it no longer felt aligned to produce them as a packaged product.

Even though I didn't want to create these bars myself, I still wanted to share them with others, and that's why I created this little book.

Why do I think this is the best recipe out there for carob bars?

I'm convinced that when NaamNom Bars were available through my website and at stores, they were among the best available of their kind. I used between 3 and 6 clean and natural ingredients (all organic), depending on the flavor, and each one was handmade. (I would also package them in compostable materials, which I didn't saw many other bar companies do. But the thought of adding thousands and thousands of little pieces of plastic to the stream of waste was not something that ever motivated me. I also packaged them by hand, which was a very, very long process; and I have hand-packed thousands of bars, myself).

The recipes are plant-based, which is a dietary and ethical part of the equation for myself and for many people.

Finally, the bars tasted like chocolate enough that many people who for various reasons could not either have certain kinds of sugars (carob contains natural sugar but is low on the glycemic index) or caffeine (the caffeine in cacao is absent from cacao butter, which is what I used— though the cacao butter still gives the texture and aroma of chocolate), could have something that met their desire for a chocolatey sweet treat. Of course, there were always people we did not win over, and some people have a challenge with cacao butter (I've suggested an alternative to that, here, in this book), but there were a bunch of people that were quite stoked that NaamNom's Carob Bars existed, and expressed sorrow to see them no longer available.

PCSD

From many anecdotal conversations with customers and potential customers for NaamNom's Carob Bars, I've gathered that sometime in the 60's or 70's or 80's, it became a fad to substitute chocolate with carob. Color does influence our experience of taste, and the color of carob is similar to chocolate. All by itself, though, the taste of carob is very different than chocolate, and it seems like not a small swath of our population was "traumatized" by bad recipes using carob. This caused what appears to be a mass aversion to the superfood. I call this (tongue-in-cheek) "PCSD", Post-Carob Stress Disorder.

With these recipes, I've done my best to reverse this aversion and transform it into appreciation for something that is delicious and nutritional, as well as an ancient superfood.

Why did I decide to make the recipes available in this book?

I love making food that brings people health and joy. Even more powerful than that is the sense of being able to spark the ability to do that, for other people.

I love demystifying foods that seem out of reach to make ourselves. For most of my life, tempered treats like chocolate were in that category. I love the potential to help do that for others, too.

I've had enough customers reach out and ask about when the bars will be available again, I want to make sure you can have them even though I will not be focusing my time on making them!

This also frees me up for more time to focus on creating illustrated children's books that touch on mindfulness and mental health (ButterflyonBooks.com), where I have a strong sense of drive and purpose right now.

Some Important Details

Where did I source my ingredients?

Here I have included direct links to the brands of each ingredient of choice that I would use. (For direct links to the ingredients, visit: Butterflyonbooks.com/carob)

Organic Carob Powder- Terrasoul
Organic Cacao Butter- Terrasoul
Pink Salt- Terrasoul
Organic Almonds- Terrasoul
Organic Walnuts- Terrasoul
Organic Mulberries- Terrasoul
Organic Cinnamon- Terrasoul
Organic Ginger- Terrasoul
Organic Deglet Noor Dates- Terrasoul
Organic Figs- Terrasoul

Organic Raisins- Bella Viva Orchards
Organic Currants- Bella Viva Orchards
Organic Pistachios- Santa Barbara
    Pistachio Company
Organic Cardamom- Spicely
Organic Peppermint- Davidson's Organic
Organic French Roasted Chicory-
    Teeccino/ Worldwide Botanicals
Organic Lavender- Anthony's

Equipment

- Food scale that will weigh to the nearest gram
- Double Boiler (A large pot over a shallow pan will suffice perfectly)
- Whisk
- Mixing Paddle
- Medium-Sized Mixing Bowls
- Food-Grade Plastic Chocolate Molds
- Food processor (for some flavors)
- Vitamix (for some flavors)
- Spoon
- Measuring cup for pouring liquids (for some flavors)

What are the "less tangible" ingredients?

Many people told me that they could always "taste the love" that I put into NaamNom's carob bars. It is a unique quality that I am grateful to have created in a dessert experience, and I attribute that to the following reasons:

» Listening to relaxing music while making the bars (you can find my playlist on Butterflyonbooks.com/carob)

» Singing while making the bars

» Focusing on my breathing and projecting a vibe of calm and love while making the bars

» If I was engaged in conversation with co-workers while making the bars, I would aspire to hold the conversation lovingly, compassionately, calmly, joyfully, and kindly.

» Being aware of my thoughts and keeping a clear head as best I could, while making the bars.

How should you use these recipes?

I give you very exact measurements here, to the gram. Feel free to play around with them if you feel inclined to! See what happens and go at it with curiosity and non-judgment.

You can feel free to multiply or divide the indicated masses depending on how many bars you'd like to make.

Make up new flavors! One of my favorite things to do is to invent new recipes. If I'd kept expanding flavors, personally, I would have added a black sesame flavored carob bar, blueberry hazelnut, maca, and others!

If you're just going to eat these bars at home, try substituting with coconut oil instead of cacao butter. It's usually less expensive and more accessible, and it stays solid when refrigerated.

Each of these recipes should make 15-25 bars, depending on the mold you use and the amount of batter you scoop or pour for each bar. This is about 1/10th to 1/20th of a typical batch size that I would make.

Note: The recipes all have similar steps, and I've erred on the side of redundancy for the sake of thoroughness.

Tempering the Bars

Tempering is what I found the most challenging part of making these bars, requiring the most skill and sensitivity. Each flavor tempers a little differently. I tempered my bars using intuition, site, and touch (I would sensitize my hand to the heat of the outside of the stainless steel pot that held the melted bar-batter).

A lot of chocolate makers use thermometers. I understand that you can also buy home tempering machines that make sure the mix is exactly the right temperature to temper perfectly. I have nothing against this, but this was not my thing. There are a lot of good videos you can easily find on YouTube if you look up "How to Temper Chocolate," and those should apply well to these recipes.

Tempering intuitively takes time to learn and even after years of practice and making thousands of bars, I do not get it 100% perfect every time. But you learn gradually, and I'm sure some of you reading this will learn how to do it more quickly than I did. Also, if you keep the bars stored in a refrigerator, you do not have to worry as much about the separation of the cacao butter and carob that can come from imperfect tempering.

Simple n Yum Carob Bar

Ingredients

500 grams carob
500 grams cacao butter
4.5 grams pink salt

Preparation

1. Measure out all the carob powder, cacao butter, and pink salt into separate bowls.

2. Melt down the cacao butter in the double-boiler. I like to boil the water first, put the flame on low, then add the cacao butter to the dry pot (or pan, for smaller quantities), then let the butter melt slowly so it does not get too hot. It helps to whisk it a bit to speed up the melting while limiting the amount of heat needed. turn off the stove as soon as the cacao butter is melted (or even before, as the heat already generated may be enough to melt the remaining cacao butter, which melts in the middle 80's Farenheit.)

3. Pour in the carob powder. (Sometimes a poof of carob powder arises from the pot when it is transferred. Feel free to cover the top for a minute to let this settle.)

4. Whisk the cacao butter, carob powder, and pink salt together.

5. Allow to cool if necessary. Pour the mixture into a measuring cup and pour to fill the molds of your choosing.

6. Mixture can be tempered at room temperature, in the refrigerator, or the freezer (fastest).

7. Enjoy!

Peppermint Carob Bar

Ingredients

450 grams carob
500 grams cacao butter
75 g peppermint leaves4.3 grams pink salt

Preparation

1. Measure out all the carob powder, cacao butter, and pink salt into separate bowls.

2. Grind peppermint leaves in a vitamix until they are a fine powder.

3. Melt down the cacao butter in the double-boiler. I like to boil the water first, put the flame on low, then add the cacao butter to the dry pot (or pan, for smaller quantities), then let the butter melt slowly so it does not get too hot. It helps to whisk it a bit to speed up the melting while limiting the amount of heat needed. turn off the stove as soon as the cacao butter is melted (or even before, as the heat already generated may be enough to melt the remaining cacao butter, which melts in the middle 80's Farenheit.)

4. Pour in the carob powder. (Sometimes a poof of carob powder arises from the pot when it is transferred. Feel free to cover the top for a minute to let this settle.)

5. Whisk the cacao butter, carob powder, and pink salt together.

6. Add the ground peppermint leaves into the mixture and whisk until smooth.

7. Allow to cool if necessary. Pour the mixture into a measuring cup and pour to fill the molds of your choosing.

8. Mixture can be tempered at room temperature, in the refrigerator, or the freezer (fastest).

9. Enjoy!

Mess-o-Pistachio Carob Bar Cardamom-Fig-Pistachio

Ingredients

475 grams carob
500 grams cacao butter
50 grams Cardamom (powdered)

500 grams figs
125 grams shelled pistachios
4.7 grams pink salt

Preparation

1. Measure out all the carob powder, cacao butter, cardamom, and pink salt into separate bowls.

2. Remove the stems from the figs and chop them into quarters. Or, put them in a food processor with a tablespoon of carob powder (so the blended fig pieces do not stick to one another) and pulse the food processor until they are the desired size (I go for the average size of a large raisin).

3. Remove the figs from the food processor and this time pour the pistachios in. Turn the food processor on for about 3 or 4 seconds, and then turn it off. (That's enough.)

4. Melt down the cacao butter in the double-boiler. I like to boil the water first, put the flame on low, then add the cacao butter to the dry pot (or pan, for smaller quantities), then let the butter melt slowly so it does not get too hot. It helps to whisk it a bit to speed up the melting while limiting the amount of heat needed. turn off the stove as soon as the cacao butter is melted (or even before, as the heat already generated may be enough to melt the remaining cacao butter, which melts in the middle 80's Farenheit.)

5. Pour in the carob powder. (Sometimes a poof of carob powder arises from the pot when it is transferred. Feel free to cover the top for a minute to let this settle.)

6. Whisk the cacao butter, carob powder, and pink salt together.

7. Whisk in the cardamom.

8. Mix in the pistachios with a spatula.

9. Mix in the figs with a spatula.

10. Allow time for cooling if necessary. Use a spoon to fill the molds of your choosing. *Note: You may need to act quickly for this step. Because of the added dried fruit and nuts, this flavor tends to temper faster than some of the others.

11. Mixture can be tempered at room temperature, in the refrigerator, or the freezer (fastest).

12. Enjoy!

Chicory Crunch Carob Bar

Ingredients

500 grams carob
500 grams cacao butter

150 g Organic French Roasted Chicory
4.5 grams pink salt

Preparation

1. Measure out all the carob powder, cacao butter, chicory, and pink salt into separate bowls.

2. Melt down the cacao butter in the double-boiler. I like to boil the water first, put the flame on low, then add the cacao butter to the dry pot (or pan, for smaller quantities), then let the butter melt slowly so it does not get too hot. It helps to whisk it a bit to speed up the melting while limiting the amount of heat needed. turn off the stove as soon as the cacao butter is melted (or even before, as the heat already generated may be enough to melt the remaining cacao butter, which melts in the middle 80's Farenheit.)

3. Pour in the carob powder. (Sometimes a poof of carob powder arises from the pot when it is transferred. Feel free to cover the top for a minute to let this settle.)

4. Whisk the cacao butter, carob powder, and pink salt together.

5. Add the chicory and mix it in with a mixing spoon, spatula, or mixing paddle.

6. Pour the mixture into a measuring cup and pour to fill the molds of your choosing.

7. Mixture can be tempered at room temperature, in the refrigerator, or the freezer (fastest).

8. Enjoy!

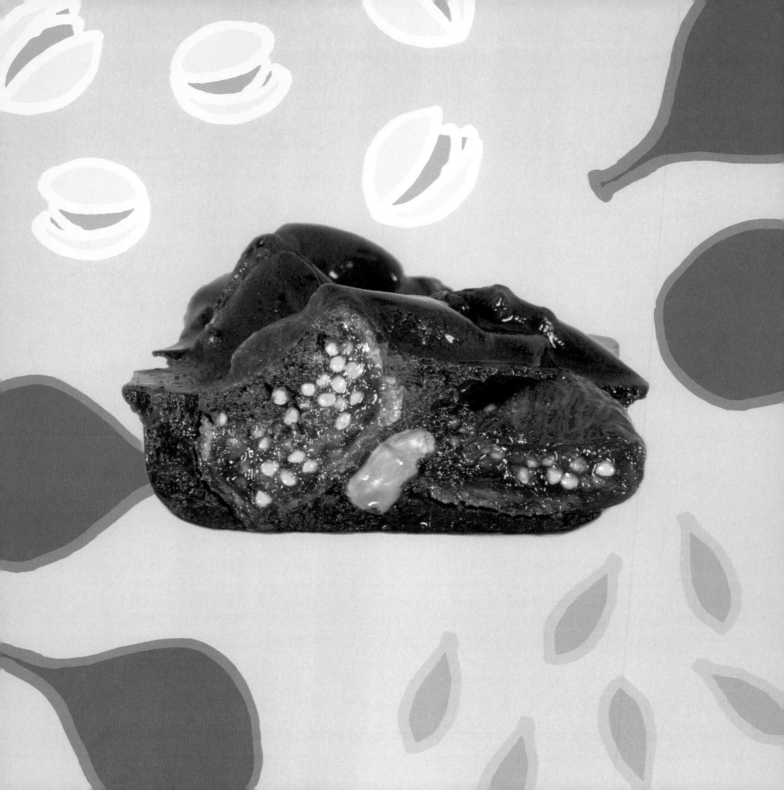

Mess-o-Pistachio Carob Bar Cardamom-Fig-Pistachio

Ingredients

475 grams carob
500 grams cacao butter
50 grams Cardamom (powdered)

500 grams figs
125 grams shelled pistachios
4.7 grams pink salt

Preparation

1. Measure out all the carob powder, cacao butter, cardamom, and pink salt into separate bowls.

2. Remove the stems from the figs and chop them into quarters. Or, put them in a food processor with a tablespoon of carob powder (so the blended fig pieces do not stick to one another) and pulse the food processor until they are the desired size (I go for the average size of a large raisin).

3. Remove the figs from the food processor and this time pour the pistachios in. Turn the food processor on for about 3 or 4 seconds, and then turn it off. (That's enough.)

4. Melt down the cacao butter in the double-boiler. I like to boil the water first, put the flame on low, then add the cacao butter to the dry pot (or pan, for smaller quantities), then let the butter melt slowly so it does not get too hot. It helps to whisk it a bit to speed up the melting while limiting the amount of heat needed. turn off the stove as soon as the cacao butter is melted (or even

before, as the heat already generated may be enough to melt the remaining cacao butter, which melts in the middle 80's Farenheit.)

5. Pour in the carob powder. (Sometimes a poof of carob powder arises from the pot when it is transferred. Feel free to cover the top for a minute to let this settle.)

6. Whisk the cacao butter, carob powder, and pink salt together.

7. Whisk in the cardamom.

8. Mix in the pistachios with a spatula.

9. Mix in the figs with a spatula.

10. Allow time for cooling if necessary. Use a spoon to fill the molds of your choosing. *Note: You may need to act quickly for this step. Because of the added dried fruit and nuts, this flavor tends to temper faster than some of the others.

11. Mixture can be tempered at room temperature, in the refrigerator, or the freezer (fastest).

12. Enjoy!

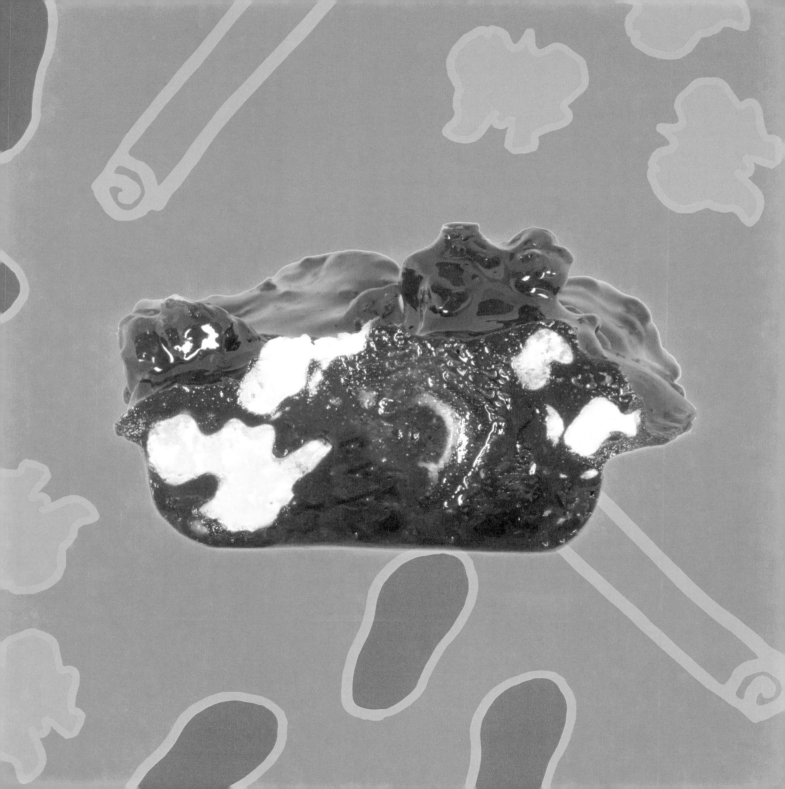

Cinnamon-Date-Walnut Carob Bar

Ingredients

475 grams carob
500 grams cacao butter
50 grams cinnamon

250 grams chopped dates
500 grams walnuts
4.8 grams pink salt

Preparation

1. Measure out all the carob powder, cacao butter, cinnamon, and pink salt into separate bowls.

2. Remove the stems and pits from the dates and chop them into quarters. Or, put them in a food processor with a tablespoon of cinnamon (so the blended date pieces do not stick to one another) and pulse the food processor until they are the desired size (I go for the average size of a large raisin).

3. Remove the dates from the food processor and this time pour the walnuts in. Turn the food processor on for about 3 or 4 seconds, and then turn it off. (That's enough.) Pour the dates into a bowl and hand-mix the rest of the cinnamon with the chopped dates.

4. Melt down the cacao butter in the double-boiler. I like to boil the water first, put the flame on low, then add the cacao butter to the dry pot (or pan, for smaller quantities), then let the butter melt slowly so it does not get too hot. It helps to whisk it a bit to speed up the melting while limiting the amount of heat needed. turn off the stove as soon as the cacao butter is melted (or even before, as the heat already generated may be enough to melt the remaining cacao butter, which melts in the middle 80's Farenheit.)

5. Pour in the carob powder. (Sometimes a poof of carob powder arises from the pot when it is transferred. Feel free to cover the top for a minute to let this settle.)

6. Whisk the cacao butter, carob powder, and pink salt together.

7. Mix in the walnuts with a spatula.

8. Mix in the date/cinnamon mixture with a spatula.

9. Allow time for cooling if necessary. Use a spoon to fill the molds of your choosing. *Note: You may need to act quickly for this step. Because of the added dried fruit and nuts, this one flavor tends to temper faster than some of the others.

10. Mixture can be tempered at room temperature, in the refrigerator, or the freezer (fastest).

11. Enjoy!

Coconut Currant Carob Bar

Ingredients

475 grams carob
500 grams cacao butter
50 grams Cardamom (powdered)

500 grams figs
125 grams shelled pistachios
4.7 grams pink salt

Preparation

1. Measure out all the carob powder, cacao butter, cardamom, and pink salt into separate bowls.

2. Remove the stems from the figs and chop them into quarters. Or, put them in a food processor with a tablespoon of carob powder (so the blended fig pieces do not stick to one another) and pulse the food processor until they are the desired size (I go for the average size of a large raisin).

3. Remove the figs from the food processor and this time pour the pistachios in. Turn the food processor on for about 3 or 4 seconds, and then turn it off. (That's enough.)

4. Melt down the cacao butter in the double-boiler. I like to boil the water first, put the flame on low, then add the cacao butter to the dry pot (or pan, for smaller quantities), then let the butter melt slowly so it does not get too hot. It helps to whisk it a bit to speed up the melting while limiting the amount of heat needed. turn off the stove as soon as the cacao butter is melted (or even before, as the heat already generated may be enough to melt the remaining cacao butter, which melts in the middle 80's Farenheit.)

5. Pour in the carob powder. (Sometimes a poof of carob powder arises from the pot when it is transferred. Feel free to cover the top for a minute to let this settle.)

6. Whisk the cacao butter, carob powder, and pink salt together.

7. Whisk in the cardamom.

8. Mix in the pistachios with a spatula.

9. Mix in the figs with a spatula.

10. Allow time for cooling if necessary. Use a spoon to fill the molds of your choosing. *Note: You may need to act quickly for this step. Because of the added dried fruit and nuts, this flavor tends to temper faster than some of the others.

11. Mixture can be tempered at room temperature, in the refrigerator, or the freezer (fastest).

12. Enjoy!

Raisin Carob Bar

Ingredients

500 grams carob
500 grams cacao butter
500 grams raisins

4.7 grams pink salt

Preparation

1. Measure out all the carob powder, cacao butter, raisins, and pink salt into separate bowls. If the raisins are clumped, unclump them.

2. Melt down the cacao butter in the double-boiler. I like to boil the water first, put the flame on low, then add the cacao butter to the dry pot (or pan, for smaller quantities), then let the butter melt slowly so it does not get too hot. It helps to whisk it a bit to speed up the melting while limiting the amount of heat needed. turn off the stove as soon as the cacao butter is melted (or even before, as the heat already generated may be enough to melt the remaining cacao butter, which melts in the middle 80's Farenheit.)

3. Pour in the carob powder. (Sometimes a poof of carob powder arises from the pot when it is transferred. Feel free to cover the top for a minute to let this settle.)

4. Whisk the cacao butter, carob powder, and pink salt together.

5. Mix in the raisins with a spatula.

6. Allow time for cooling if necessary. Use a spoon to fill the molds of your choosing. *Note: You may need to act quickly for this step. Because of the added dried fruit, this flavor tends to temper faster than some of the others. Also, the raisins have a tendency to sink to the bottom of the pot. Make sure when you go into the mixture with the spoon, go to the bottom of the pot.

7. The mixture can be tempered at room temperature, in the refrigerator, or the freezer (fastest).

8. Enjoy!

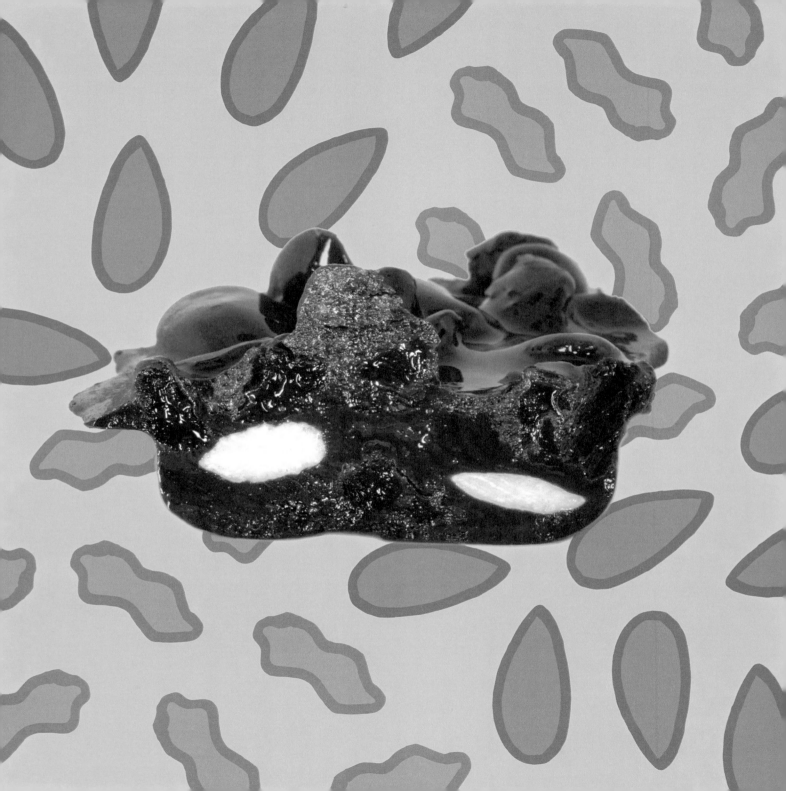

Almond-Raisin Carob Bar

Ingredients

500 grams carob
500 grams cacao butter
375 grams almonds

375 grams raisins
4.8 grams pink salt

Preparation

1. Measure out all the carob powder, cacao butter, raisins, and pink salt into separate bowls. If raisins are clumped, unclump them.

2. Optional: Spread out almonds on a baking sheet and roast them at 250 degrees Fahrenheit for 15-20 minutes, or as desired. Also option: pulse the almonds in a food processor for about 5 seconds, or to desired size.

3. Melt down the cacao butter in the double-boiler. I like to boil the water first, put the flame on low, then add the cacao butter to the dry pot (or pan, for smaller quantities), then let the butter melt slowly so it does not get too hot. It helps to whisk it a bit to speed up the melting while limiting the amount of heat needed. turn off the stove as soon as the cacao butter is melted (or even before, as the heat already generated may be enough to melt the remaining cacao butter, which melts in the middle 80's Farenheit.)

4. Pour in the carob powder. (Sometimes a poof of carob powder arises from the pot when it is transferred. Feel free to cover the top for a minute to let this settle.)

5. Whisk the cacao butter, carob powder, and pink salt together.

6. Mix in the almonds with a spatula.

7. Mix in the raisins with a spatula.

8. Allow time for cooling if necessary. Use a spoon to fill the molds of your choosing.*Note: You may need to act quickly for this step. Because of the added dried fruit and nuts, this flavor tends to temper faster than some of the others.

9. Mixture can be tempered at room temperature, in the refrigerator, or the freezer (fastest).

10. Enjoy!

Mulberry Ginger Carob Bar

Ingredients

475 grams carob
500 grams cacao butter
500 grams mulberries

25 grams ginger
4.7 grams pink salt

Preparation

1. Measure out all the carob powder, cacao butter, ginger, and pink salt into separate bowls.

2. Spread the mulberries on a baking sheet lined with parchment paper. Roast them for 20 minutes at 225 degrees Fahrenheit, for 20 minutes or until the mulberries around the edges are golden brown.

3. While the mulberries are cooling, melt down the cacao butter in the double-boiler. I like to boil the water first, put the flame on low, then add the cacao butter to the dry pot (or pan, for smaller quantities), then let the butter melt slowly so it does not get too hot. It helps to whisk it a bit to speed up the melting while limiting the amount of heat needed. turn off the stove as soon as the cacao butter is melted (or even before, as the heat already generated may be enough to melt the remaining cacao butter, which melts in the middle 80's Farenheit.)

4. Pour in the carob powder. (Sometimes a poof of carob powder arises from the pot when it is transferred. Feel free to cover the top for a minute to let this settle.)

5. Whisk the cacao butter, carob powder, and pink salt together.

6. Whisk in the ginger.

7. Mix in the mulberries with a spatula.

8. Allow time for cooling if necessary. Use a spoon to fill if necessary. Use a spoon to fill the molds of your choosing.*Note: You may need to act quickly for this step. Because of the added dried fruit, this flavor tends to temper faster than some of the others.

9. Mixture can be tempered at room temperature, in the refrigerator, or the freezer (fastest).

10. Enjoy!

Contact

I'd love to connect with you! Please feel free to find me on instagram through **@oshrihakak** or to email me at **oshri@butterflyonbooks.com**.

Thank Yous

Thank you to my family, and to Grace Jolicoeur, Rachel Silverman, Hillary Barker, Ricardo Mendoza, Alex Buell, and Dohnbi Kim for your support with making NaamNom happen.

More Titles from Butterflyon Books

visit ButterflyonBooks.com

**Deep Breathing
is My Blanket**
by Oshri

Hamsa the Butterfly
by Oshri

Blagalaga
by Oshri

Draw-Wings

Draw-Wings
by Oshri

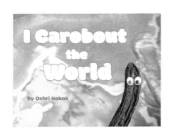

I Carobout the World
by Oshri

Happy Minutes
by Oshri

Okels & Wokels
by Oshri and Art &
James Mihaley

The Child in Me
By Oshri

Tending The Tumlin
Words by Oshri and Art
by Gordon Motsinger

When I Listen
by Oshri

Shimmer & Glint
by The Brother's Grin

All Kinds of Hugs
by Oshri

**Listen to the Land:
A Tale of Two Flowers**
by Oshri

30

Printed in the USA
CPSIA information can be obtained
at www.ICGtesting.com
LVRC091235030524
779175LV00005B/11